Up to t[illegible] Stars

Written by Jill Atkins
Illustrated by Bernice Lum

RIGBY

Dad gets a red and brown carpet.
Cora and Mark sit on it.

The carpet lifts up!
“Wow! We are going up high.”

The carpet zooms down, then up,
up ... up to the stars.

Cora and Mark go to far-off lands.

Cora points. “Look, a shark!”

It snaps its sharp teeth at her.

Mark and Cora see big cats prowling.

They see a man selling carpets in a crowded market.

It gets dark.
The wind starts to howl.

Mark and Cora go into the storm.

The carpet tosses and turns.

Mark turns on his torch.

But Mum and Dad will miss us. We must go back soon.

The carpet is back in the
sitting room.

Cool carpet, Dad!